THE DEVIL OF DARKNESS
in the
LIGHT OF EVOLUTION.

by

Gerald Massey

There are two things which I have come to look upon as constituting the *unpardonable* sin of the father and mother against the helpless innocence of infancy. The one is in allowing their little children to run the risk of blood-poisoning--such as was once suffered by a child of mine--from the *filthy fraud of vaccination*. The other is in permitting the mind and soul of their children to be inoculated with the still more fatal virus of the old, false, orthodox dogmas and delusions, by allowing them to believe that the fables of ancient mythology are the sacred and solely true "Word of God," if they are found in the Hebrew Scriptures--the one book of the religiously ignorant. Generation after generation we learn, unlearn, and relearn the same lying, legendary lore, and it takes the latter half of all one's lifetime to throw off the mass of corrupting error instilled into us during the earlier half, even when we do break out and slough it off in a mental eruption, and *have* to find ourselves in utter rebellion against things as they are. Unfortunately, the mass of people never do get rid of this infection, nor of the desire to give their disease to others.

The fact of the matter is, the Christian dogmas and doctrines began as such with being unintelligible and inexplicable; they were to remain as mysteries; and any true explanation of them is death to their false pretentions. It is my method to explode by explaining them. Take the doctrine of the Trinity for example. Can any theologian throughout all Christendom to-day give us any intelligible account of its origin and primary meaning? Not one. For that we must go to mythology, which was earlier than our theology, and which alone enables us to explain its primitive mysteries. The natural genesis of the Trinity was found, and is to be refound, in lunar phenomena. The moon, in mythology and chronology, was a time-measurer of a three-fold nature. At fifteen days of age, or full-moon, it was the mother-moon. Hence Ishtar, in Akkad, is designated Goddess 15. The lessening, waning moon was her little one, the child of the moon, who became the virile one, the adult, as the horned new moon, the reproducer who was fabled to rebeget himself on the mother moon, and thus become his own father, as a natural mode of describing natural phenomena.

These three *are* eternally *one* in external nature--a Trinity always manifesting monthly, and the triple aspect was humanly, or naturally, expressed by means of the mother, child, and reproducing male, which three are also one in the total human being. In the Christian Iconography, you will sometimes see the Virgin Mary enthroned in the new moon, with the child in her arms, and these two, with the horned or phallic moon, constitute the Christian Trinity in Unity. Such was the primitive mode of thinking in things, afterwards continued in a mystical or doctrinal phase. *Such,* I affirm to be the *origin* of the Trinity in mythology, which preceded religion; and when this is applied abstractly, to the nature of deity, or to mind in nature, by means of metaphysic, the result is an imposition, and he or she who practices imposition, consciously or not, is an impostor. No such thing can be known as a triune or triangular God; but we are able to show how such types originated. When our words are examined, we shall frequently find that our metaphysic has been abstracted, or falsely filched from primitive physics, as was the Trinity by Plato, which was continued by the Christian Fathers, who tell us that but for Plato they would never have understood the doctrine of the Trinity. As with the Trinity, so it is with the origin of the theological Devil. The crucial question of the savage man, Friday, was too fundamental for the theology of Robinson Crusoe. Friday asks, "But, if God much strong, much mighty as the devil, why God no kill the devil, and so make him no more wicked?" Crusoe, imitating other theologists, not knowing what to say, "pretended not to hear him." (I am told this passage has been omitted from certain recent editions.) To give an answer to that question we shall have to go round to work. It would never do to begin a lecture on this subject like the well-known chapter headed "Snakes in Iceland," which consisted of the statement, "there are no snakes in Iceland!" If I did, my lecture might be summed up in the words, "there is no devil." But every belief, superstition, and mental type, had its natural genesis once, the devil included.

The result of 14 years' research in the Records of the Past is a personal conviction that the human mind has long suffered an eclipse, and been darkened and dwarfed in the shadow of ideas, the real meaning of which has been lost to the moderns! Myths and allegories, whose significance was once unfolded to the initiates in the ancient mysteries, have been adopted in ignorance, and re-issued as real truths divinely vouchsafed to mankind for the first and only time when found in the Hebrew writings! The earlier religions had their myths interpreted by means of the oral and unwritten Wisdom. We have ours *misinterpreted;* and a great deal of what has been imposed upon us as God's direct, true, and sole revelation to man, is a mass of *inverted myths,* under the shadow of which men have been cowering as timorously as birds in the stubble, when a kite in the shape of a hawk is held hovering overhead to keep them down; as I have seen it practised in England!

The parables and types of the primeval thinkers have been elevated to the "Sphere," as the "hawk," or "serpent," the "bull," or the "crab," that give names to certain groups of stars, and we are precisely in the same relationship to these religious parables and allegories as we should be to astronomical facts, if we thought the serpent and bull, lion, sea-goat, and ram were real animals up in heaven, instead of constellations with symbolical names. The Jews picked up various traditions of other races. Moses, they tell us, was an initiate in all the learning of the Egyptians. And these myths have been so handled as to efface their primitive features altogether. They have been so "sweated" down, by later theologies, to make capital--get gold-dust, as it were, out of them--that they can only be recognised by comparison with the earlier copies yet extant among other nations, from which the Jews derived their versions.

Fossil remains, found in the lowermost strata of human thought, have been preserved as divine patterns for the ignorant and superstitious of later ages. The simple realities of the earliest times were expressed by signs and symbols, and these have been taken and applied to later thought, and converted into theological problems and metaphysical mysteries, for which our theologians have no basis whatever, and can only wrangle over *en l'air;* they cannot touch solid earth with one foot when they want to kick opponents with the other; and when they try to bite you very viciously they find that they have only been furnished with a set of teeth that are false. The only possible way of exposing the false pretensions of theological dogmas is by explaining them from the root, and showing what they meant as mythos. The orthodox teaching which is founded on the "Fall of Man," is shattered, even as a pane of glass is fractured at a blow, when once we can apply the Doctrine of Development.

The Hebrew devil, or Satan, means the opponent or adversary, and the first great natural adversary recognised by primitive man was Darkness--simply darkness, the constant and eternal enemy of the light--that is, the power of darkness was literal before it became metaphorical, moral, or spiritual.

Hence darkness itself was the earliest devil or adversary, the obstructor and deluder of man, the eternal enemy of the sun. We speak of the "jaws of darkness;" and darkness was the vast, huge, swallower of the light, night after night. We know this was identified as the primary power, because the primitive or early man reckoned time by nights, and the years by Eclipses. This mode of reckoning was first and universal. So many darks preceded so many days. The dark power is primarily in all the oldest traditions and cults of the human race. Hence sacrifice was first offered to the powers of darkness. The fore-words of universal mythology are "there was darkness." All was dark at first within the mind; and the *all was* the *darkness* that created dread without. The influence of night, the eclipse, and the black thunder-cloud being first felt, the primitive man visibly emerges from the shadow of darkness as deeply impressed and indelibly dyed in mind as was his body with its natural blackness. The black man without was negroid within, as his reflection remains in the mirror of mythology. The darkness then, in natural phenomena, was the original devil that put out the light by swallowing it incessantly, as the subtle enemy, the obstructor, deluder, and general adversary of man. The first form of the Devil was female, called the Dragon of Darkness, who was Tiamat in Akkad, and Typhon in Egypt. Typhon gave birth to Sut, who became the Egyptian devil--our Satan--and who was represented by the Black jackal, the voice of Darkness; and Sut, the black one, gives us the name of Soot, the black thing. Angro-Mainyus, the Persian devil, was the black one of the two powers of Light and Darkness.

Primitive man, however, did not imagine or personify a devil behind visible phenomena, that caused the darkness. Darkness itself was the devil, and even as late as the Parsee Bundahish (which means the aboriginal creation) external darkness is the devil.

The seven devils or seven heads of the old Dragon, in the Akkadian myths of creation, are born in the mountains of sunset, which shows the same natural genesis in physical phenomena. They had their *birth-place* where the sun went down. At the same place, in the West, the Egyptians stationed the Great Crocodile that swallowed down the lights, sun, moon, and stars, as they set each night, in its wide-open jaws of darkness. Hence the crocodile was an ideograph of the swallowing darkness--and of earth, or the waters below, called the Abyss; and the tail of the crocodile remained in the Egyptian hieroglyphics as the sign of Kam -- that is, of blackness or darkness. The crocodile was the typical Dragon of the waters below, the old Typhon, as the serpent was of the waters, or overwhelming darkness, above. Hor-Apollo tells us the Egyptians represent the mouth by a serpent, because the serpent is all mouth. This was another figure of the swallower, as the Akhekh and the Apap serpent. Akhekh signifies darkness, and Apap means that which rises up vast and gigantic-- in short, the monster--the typical Apap being based on the great African rock-snake. Here, then, is the reason why the mythical dragon and the old serpent are identical or interchangeable in mythology, each being a representative of the devil of darkness and of Satan, that old serpent, who imaged the evil which was first perceived in physical phenomena. Out of the darkness leapt the lightning-bolt, and in the deep waters lurked another subtle foe of life, and thus the jaws, the fang, and the sting of death were assigned to the devil of darkness, who gradually assumed the character of man's mortal enemy that brought death into the world. The course of this development can be traced from the beginning, in physical darkness, to the culmination, in a psycho-theistic phase, for everything yields to an application of the evolutionary method--and you may depend upon it that evolution has come into the world to stay; and evolution and the Hebrew genesis cannot co-exist in the same mental world.

The earliest mode of representing the eternal alternation of external phenomena called night and day, or darkness and light, the good and bad, is to be found in the universal myth of the Two Brothers, who are born twins,--very imperfect versions of which may be found in the legends of Cain and Abel, and of Esau and Jacob. In this myth, the Dark and Day are born twins of the Great Mother, and these brothers are pourtrayed as always being at enmity with each other, and in conflict before their birth, as are the darkness and the light when struggling at dawn! They fight one another in the effort of each to get born first. This becomes the well-known struggle of the birthright, which is universal in mythology. Far more perfect versions of the same mythos are extant among the blacks of Australia, the Red Indians of America, the Bushmen and Hottentots of Africa, more perfect, because simpler, nearer to nature, and less moralized. It is the myth of Sut-Horus in Egypt. Sut-Horus is the dual manifestor of dark and light, who is depicted with the double head of the black vulture of night and the golden hawk of light, upon one body. The dark one was born first, because darkness was first cognised; but they both continued to struggle for supremacy after birth, as they had done before it, because they dramatised the ceaseless and endless alternation of night and day, of dark and light, seen in the heavens at eve and dawn, in the orb of the moon, and the lengthening of darkness, or of light, in autumn and in spring! Here again the dark power is the devil, the bad dev, and the light is the good power, the bright dev.

The same conflict, based upon the alternation of light and darkness, is pourtrayed as the struggle of St. George, our solar hero, who conquers the dragon just as Horus overthrows the Apap dragon upon the monuments of Egypt. And when the devil's knell is rung annually at Horbury, in Yorkshire, England, *that* is in celebration of the death of the Dragon of Darkness; and the same custom is also continued in ringing out the old year, on the last night in December. When in New South Wales I picked up a tradition of the blacks. The Devil, called Mullion, lived in a very tall tree, at Girra, on the Barwon river, and used to eat black fellows! They tried to burn down this vast tree, in which the Devil of darkness dwelt, but the fires were always put out by invisible spirits. Then they got a red mouse, put a lighted straw in his mouth, and started him up the tree. The loose bark caught fire, the tree blazed for weeks, the devil was burned out, and never came back again. This red mouse is also a type of Horus in Egypt. Naturally, then, the devil of darkness was the first divinity, because the dark power is primal! When it came to worshipping, or, rather, to propitiating, by offering the fruits of fear, it was the dark power that predominated, because this struck terror and elicited fear. *"Primos in orbe deos fecit timor!"* Sometimes these twins of darkness and light are called the ugly and beautiful brothers. And here the persistence of the mythical types may be noticed, for these two are not only continued as the Sut-Horus, or double Horus of Egypt, but they are likewise extant in that museum of mythical types, the Catacombs of Rome, as the Twin-Christs, one of which is pourtrayed as the beautiful youth; the other is the little, old, and ugly Christ. Just as it was in the pre-Christian times, from which these figures were a Gnostic survival.

Next, Mind becomes an element in the manifestation of phenomena; and in the American myths, the born twins are called the bad mind and the good mind. In this phase the twin-brothers are not only mental, they are also moralized on their way to becoming the dual divinity, or modern God and Devil. In the

Avesta, and other Persian Scriptures, for example, the twin-brothers can be traced from the Natural Genesis in phenomena, as light and darkness, to their becoming personified as divinity and devil, in Ahura-Mazda, the God of mental light, and Angro-Mainyus, the devil of mental darkness. Here the older bogey of the night has been found out! Men had dipped into the dark, and suffered from the shadow of eclipse so long, and passed through them so often and so safely, that their essential unreality was discovered at last. Thus Angro-Mainyus, the black mind, is only accredited with the creation of all that is untrue, unreal, and utterly delusive in nature. The light had now become the enduring reality, and darkness was only its deluding shadow. They now recognised that the dark one in the physical, mental, or moral domain, was only negative and negational; the bright one, the god of light, the good mind, was the Supreme Being, the reality, therefore the author of all that was finally real and eternally true! These are the two causes of the universe--it is said;--they were united from the Beginning, and, therefore, are called the *Twins,* and the Persian "Revelation" contains the Gnosis and explanation of the doctrine concerning these twin spirits.

Such was the natural origin of that doctrine of duality, which is discussed now-a-days as a metaphysical mystery, and as if it *were* a reality from the root of it, made known to the world by direct revelation! The origin of Good and Evil in the nature of man considered as a being of flesh and spirit, as the personal embodiment of two opposite principles, assumed to have a spontaneous or automatic tendency towards good on the part of the one which is supposed to originate in the spirit, and the other to originate in the flesh, as a natural antagonist, is traceable to this most primitive interpretation of the duality called good and evil in external phenomena, which was continued in the mental and moral, and lastly in the psycho-theistic phase of thought. In its latest stage the doctrine is destructive of individual responsibility in man and of personal unity in deity, or the operating Intelligence. There was no revelation, no new point of departure in phenomena, nothing added to nature or human knowledge in these later views of mythology into metaphysic, philosophy, or theology, in which the supposed revelation of newer truth was largely founded on a falsification of the old.

We are not only contemporaries of savage men in many of our current customs and benighting beliefs, we are also the victims of his leavings--various of our superstitions being the primitive fetishism that still survives in the last stage of perversion.

But now for a development of the Devil!

In Egypt the old Devil of darkness, as Sut-Typhon or Sevekh, the Crocodile-headed divinity, acquired a soul in the stars and a place in heaven, as Plutarch says. To him was given the Crocodile or Dragon Constellation in the planisphere, whose casting out of heaven is described in the Book of Revelation, and in the Persian Bahman Yasht, where Sut, or Sevekh the Dragon, that old serpent, is identified as Satan, the eternal adversary of souls, just as it is in the Egyptian Ritual of the Dead. Thus, the devil that first rose up in revolt, as the natural darkness, called the Dragon of the deep, the rebel against the light-god, was gradually transformed into a supposed starry or spiritual being, the vice-dieu of the dark, who, in the Christian scheme, is still considered to be the supreme power of the two, or if their dominions be equally divided, he is supreme below and the light-god above--just as it had been from the beginning. And, finally, our theology has made the primal shadow of physical phenomena substantial in the mental sphere, and from the external darkness of that beginning extracted and internalised the modern devil in the end!

I have now given you a sample of what I meant by our being in the shadow of ideas whose original signification we have not understood.

There is no devil such as Milton saw! And as you must know, much current theology has been derived from "Paradise Lost." The hawk that has been flying or flown to keep timid souls cowering down to the ground, is not the real bird of prey after all. You may trace every motion of it to the end of the string held in the puller's hand! When you go close up to it, the devil of theology is not alive. It is a bogus bug-bear, hideous, but harmless as that scarecrow in the field, the imposture of which had been found out and despised by a small bird who had built its nest, and laid and hatched its eggs in one of the grim monster's waistcoat pockets.

We have an old saying that the devil is an ass! But, in Egypt, the devil as Sut or Satan was the ass--the ass that carried the Christ as Horus, the saviour. This was the ass that was figuratively kicked out in the Christian sport of "beating the ass," when that pastime used to be practised up and down the aisles of Christian churches, and the priest used to bray three times, and the people responded like asses!

The German devil was at one time the red-bearded thunder, the Voice of Darkness! which takes us back to Sut-Typhon, who, as Plutarch informs us, was of a reddish complexion. It is common for our giants to be endowed with a red streaming comet's tail of a beard! Our forefathers, the Norsemen, had little respect and no reverence for the devil; and as to hell, why, if you did not get to heaven, then hell was the next best place in the other world, if there were but two!

To be sure, they were badly off for firewood in the Norse hell; and spirits sat shivering in the presence of the cold, uncomfortable goddess Hela, who was blue with cold, and it was trying to think how they were keeping it up overhead--they who had climbed to the top of the tree, Ygdrasil, or secured a seat in Valhalla where the wine-cups flowed and the fagots flared, and the merry dancing flames might be reflected on the windows of a heaven that was closed against them. For the North-Men knew nothing of a hell of everlasting fire. If they had, it might have proved the more attractive place of the two; as one of our missionaries once discovered. He had gone out to Greenland to carry the Gospel of Good Tidings, and illustrate it with the aid of an eternal fire! But he found himself in the wrong latitude as regards the effect of fire. He pictured it in the warmest colours, and was surprised at the result! Instead of seeing awe and terror whitening their faces, or the tears trickling down them, as he had expected, they were blubbering in quite another fashion, for the whale's fat began to run and glisten on their relaxed faces, which he saw rounding and brightening into full moons of happiness and jollity; and instead of wringing their hands at the prospect he had pictured, they sat as if spiritually warming them at this "everlasting bonfire," that was so earnestly warranted never to go out!

If this were the gospel of good tidings, why had they not heard the glorious truth before? Such a welcome and delightful change from the life they had lived in their inclement, wintry climate! They had never dreamed of conditions so delightful! So far from shunning such a place for ever, as he desired them to do, they were quite ready and willing, all of them to go to it at once, and stay there forever.

The mythical devil was pretty much dying out, until it was revived and sublimated by the theology of Luther, Calvin, and Milton. The Romish Church did not deify the devil as the Protestants have done. She was better acquainted with the tradition of his creation and the earthly nature of his character. It was her cue to keep dark. And the devil of the Middle Ages is a poor devil enough without grandeur or terror! A very fallen intelligence, indeed, whom Romish saints can tweak by the nose with red-hot tongs, or the simplest countrymen have cunning enough to outwit. Instead of the arch-enemy of God and man, majestic in his dark divinity, infernally inspired, as Milton pictures him, he has become a grotesque image; the story-teller's most popular figure of fun, on a par with the giants of our nursery lore, whom the clever, redoubtable, little Jack, always gets the better of! Indeed, both devil and giant as well as the serpent and dragon, had one origin, and the orthodox Satan is, after all, the popular monster of mythology. Luther and Calvin doubled the devil, and placed one at each end of their scheme of things, the upper or bright God being rather the worse devil of the two!

They put the doctrine of dualism as perplexingly as did the negro preacher who told his congregation there were but two roads open to them--one of these led directly to destruction, and the other went straight to perdition. "Stop a bit, brudder," cried one of the congregation; "hold hard, whilst I get out ob dis!" And there are many people who desire to become followers of that negro, and "get out ob dis."

The Satan of sacerdotal belief, then, is not a being for God or man to kill, but an effigy in shoddy that only wants to be ripped up to show you that it is stuffed with sawdust!

Some people may cry out in an agony of earnestness, as Charles Lamb stammered in his fun, "But this is doing away with the devil; d-d-d-don't deprive me of my devil!" "We hope for better things. How shall we be able to force people into thinking as we do, and frighten them into *our* fold of faith, for the glory of God, if we have no devil for our ferocious shepherd-dog?" And there is no doubt but that, in giving up the orthodox Hell and ancient Devil, we are losing one of the most potent motive powers. Our difficulty is how to find a substitute for the appeal to selfish fear. The fact remains that the devil is a fundamental part of the Christian scheme! No devil, no Redeemer! And those who will yell at me, and call me a blasphemer, know that well enough. I sympathise with them. They begin to see dimly, what we see clearly, that orthodox Christianity is answerable with its life for the literal truth of these stories of the Devil, the Fall of man, and the doctrine of a dying deity's atonement. Its life is *staked* upon the stories being *true;* and its life must pay the forfeit of their being found to be false! And false they are, however their defenders may squirm and wriggle, until the backbone of all manhood is changed into caoutchouc(rubber).

I can imagine that people who are not sure of their own souls, whether they are lost or are not yet found, unless their Hebrew Genesis be true, will feel the world is a rather hollow affair without their accustomed devil. It will be like depriving them of half their heaven on earth, and the whole of it hereafter, to take away the devil. What on earth, or in another place, will they do? those who are so virulent by nature for the Calvinistic sulphur, if, after all, there is no brimstone there; and they have passed out of this life with their itch for hell red-hot upon them, and there is no Old Scratch to console them after all? One would like to believe in just a very little hell for their dear sake! They have so devoutly believed in a big one for ours.

There *is* devil enough, however--only of another kind than the one we have played with. We have talked of the devil long enough; but to a Spiritualist, for instance, the devil exists for the first time in some of the facts made known by modern Spiritualism--facts which are as much matters of personal experience and constant verification to myself and myriads of others as are those of your ordinary life! Think for a moment tentatively of there being a personal motive on the other side--a vested interest in our wrong doing--degraded spirits present with us in the enjoyment of our most secret sins--the ghosts of old dead drunkards haunting the drinker's live warm atmosphere, because in that there may pass off into spirit-world some ghostly gust of the old delirious delight, and you may get at a real, present, self-interested, manifold, tempting devil that altogether surpasses the mythological monster of theology!

The devil and hell of my creed consist in that natural Nemesis which follows on broken laws, and dogs the law breaker, in spite of any belief of his, that his sins, and their inevitable results can be so cheaply sponged out, as he has been misled to think, through the shedding of innocent blood. Nature knows nothing of the forgiveness for sin. She has no rewards or punishments--nothing but causes and consequences. For example, if you should contract a certain disease and pass it on to your children, and their children, all the alleged forgiveness of God will be of no avail if you cannot forgive yourself. Ours is the devil of heredity, working in two worlds at once. Ours is a far more terrible way of realising the hereafter, when it is brought home to us in concrete fact, whether in this life or the life to come, than any abstract idea of hell or devil can afford. We have to face the facts beforehand. No use to whine over them impotently afterwards, when it is too late. For example—

In the olden days when Immortals
To earth came visible down,
There went a youth with an Angel
Through the gate of an Eastern town:
They passed a dog by the road-side,
Where dead and rotting it lay,
And the youth, at the ghastly odour,
Sickened and turned away.
He gathered his robes about him;
And hastily hurried thence:
But nought annoyed the Angel's
Clear, pure, immortal sense.
By came a lady, lip-luscious,
On delicate, mincing feet:
All the place grew glad with her presence,
All the air about her sweet;
For she came in fragrance floating,
And her voice most silvery rang;
And the youth, to embrace her beauty,
With all his being sprang.
A sweet, delightsome lady:
And yet, the Legend saith,
The Angel, while he passed her,
Shuddered and held his breath!

Only think of a fine lady who, in this life, has been wooed and flattered, sumptuously clad, and delicately fed; for whom the pure, sweet, air of heaven had to be perfumed as incense! and the red rose of health had to fade from many young human faces to blossom in the robes she wore, and every sense had been most daintily feasted, and her whole life summed up in one long thought of self--think of her finding herself in the next life a spiritual leper, a walking pestilence, a personified disease--a sloughing sore of this life which the spirit has to get rid of--an excrement of this life's selfishness at which all good spirits stop their noses and shudder when she comes near! Don't you think if she realised that as a fact in time, it would work more effectually than much preaching? The hell of the drunkard, the libidinous, the blood-thirsty, or gold-greedy soul, they tell us, is the burning of the old devouring passion which was *not* quenched by the chills of death. The crossing of the cold, dark river even was only as the untasted water to the consuming thirst of Tantalus! In support of this, evolution shows the continuity of ourselves, our desires, passions, and characters. As the Egyptians said, Whoso is intelligent here will be intelligent there! And if we haven't mastered and disciplined our lower passions here, they will be masters of us for the time-being hereafter.

There is no such possibility as death-bed salvation! No such thing as being *"jerked to Jesus"* if you are converted on the scaffold!

These old passions of ours burn and burn, and will and must burn on till they burn out. That, they tell us, is as absolutely necessary a process in the spiritual world as in the case of a fever in the physical body, which may be fed frightfully by the impurities of the previous life. Moreover, the fever will rage so long as it is supplied with fresh fuel. So long as the infatuated spirit does not try to put out the fire, and give the spiritual nature its one chance of throwing off the infernal disease, but lusts in imagination after that which fed the flame at first, and stirs the fire that kindles with every sigh for the old flesh-pots of evil passion still; and will come back to earth to prowl in filthy places, and snuff the ill odours of the lowest animal life; seeking in vain for some gust of satisfaction in shadowy apparition, as a spirit earth-bound, and self-bound to earth. Such is the teaching inculcated by our facts, accept or reject them whosoever may!

For, where the treasure is there will the heart be also. Think of that, you treasure-seekers in the earth, who have found and laid your treasures on the earth; whose treasures represent the life you have spent on the earth! You have put the better part of your life into them. They *are* your better part. But you cannot take them away with you! The only treasure we can carry away with us must be laid up within. Now, Spiritualism reveals the possibility of the spirit's being doomed to haunt this treasure-house of earth until every particle of that hoarded wealth has been redistributed and restored to the channels for which it was intended by the Maker, and the first stage on its way back may be that the riches so carefully gathered and miserly garnered shall be the means of sinking your spendthrift son down to the lowest range of spiritual penury. For the Creator whom we postulate will not be baulked in carrying out his purposes by any temporary obstructions like these, and if you have hindered here you will have to help hereafter, when you do at last get into line with Natural *Law*.

You have been amused with a dolly devil long enough, whilst inside of you, and outside of you, and all round about you, the real devil is living, working with a most infernal activity, and playing the very devil with this world of ours. Not an ideal devil, but a legal devil, with a purpose and a plan; *the* devil in reality!

We have been following a phantom of faith, and the actual veritable devil has been dogging us indeed! This is not a Satan of God's making. Not an archangel ruined, who, in falling, found a foothold on this earth for the purpose of dragging men down with him to that lower deep for which he is bound, but a devil to be recognised by his likeness to ourselves! the devil that *is* our worser self! the devil of our own ignorance, and the deification of self--a devil bequeathed to us by the accumulated gains of centuries of ignorant selfishness, and selfish ignorance--a devil to be grappled with and wrestled with and throttled, overthrown, and overcome, and put out of existence--not only in the struggle against all that is evil in the isolated, individual life; our devil has grown too big and is too potent for that; but by the energies of all collected and clubbed, and made co-operant to destroy the causes of evil whensoever and wheresoever these can be identified, whether as Religious, or Political, Moral, or Social. We stand in Heaven's own light and cast the evil shadow of Self, and say it is the devil. And then our theologians have the blasphemous impudence to make God the author of this dark shadow of ourselves, which we shed on his creation; and assume it to be an eclipse from another world of Being.

No doubt it may be shown that the Operative Power we postulate is responsible for certain natural conditions which inevitably result in what we recognise to be evil. Nor will he shirk his responsibility in that matter. It was a necessary part and process in the human education, in strict accordance with the laws of evolution. But we see more and more every day that such evil was good in the making. We may trace many of the healing springs of heavenly purity filtering through this dark stratum of earth. Also, we are apt to look on things at first sight as evil which we finally find to be blessings in disguise. A piercing vision will perceive the deeply underlying intention of good working upward through many a superficial appearance of evil. Seen in the light of Evolution, the existence of evil is no longer a mythological mystery to be made the most of by pious ignoramuses for preaching purposes, but a necessary concomitant of development; one of the conditions by means of which we grow into conscious human beings to attain the higher life.

Indeed, whether there be a God or not, it was impossible to discuss the matter intelligently until the doctrine of Creation, by the slow processes of evolution, had been taken into account.

This shows us that the evil for which Nature is responsible, is a means of evolving in us the very consciousness of good. The moment we recognise evil, and have acquired the consciousness of its existence, the responsibility for its existence becomes ours. Here is a problem set for us to solve by way of education. Here is a foe to fight to the death, whether as a misguided passion in the individual, or a disease in the life of a nation. Here is something to be turned into good--a devil to be converted. The moment man sees so far, *he* must accept the responsibility for the continued existence of the evil, and war against it as he would if clearing any other jungle from poisonous reptiles. Ours is not a doll to dandle, and claim divine parentage for, but a misbegotten devil of ignorance, and a miscarriage of humanity in the past.

We see that life comes into visible being according to conditions. Where these are unprepared and not humanised, the life takes the lowest forms, those of reptiles and weeds, poisonous plants, thorns, thistles, and briars, forms inimical to man, and therefore considered to be evil. Then man comes to cultivate and modify, and turn the evil into good. The whole world of natural evil has to acknowledge its master. Let me give you an illustration. Pain, for example, is a consequence of imperfect conditions. It is the signal of the sentinel that warns us of the enemy. And how those faithful sentinels stand in the outworks of the body, to guard the more vital parts from approaching danger. It is necessary to warn us, or we should do most foolish things, as a child might, but for this warning of pain, thrust his hand in the fire and have it consumed! The soul's health is continually protected by this warning sentinel of pain, mental and corporeal. Pain is necessary, then, to the development of consciousness, and the perfecting of conditions. It is the reminder that there is something wrong; therefore something to be remedied. It is a part of the process in our education. Also, the loftiest pleasures of our spiritual life continually flower from a rootage in the deepest pain. I am not here to preach a gospel of the blessedness of suffering for the poor and needy -- the victims of this world's laws. But suffering, as I read the Book of Life, is an incentive to effort; and the greatest pressure from without will sometimes evolve the strongest character from within, by evoking the greater force of effort. As Shakespeare points out, the flowers of March are not so fine as the flowers of June, but the finest flower of March is finer than the finest flower of June! It has overcome more opposition, and turned it to account. Perhaps in consequence of the pressure, it has established a nearer relationship at root to the source of life. Pain is but a passing necessity, for, as it is the result of imperfect conditions, it follows that pain itself must pass away as those conditions are perfected-- and *we* are here to improve and perfect them. God does not destroy the devil of pain right off, by working a miracle at a moment's notice! For God is not that Automaton of the sects-- that weather-cock atop of creation which they suppose will veer round at every breath of selfish prayer. You are called upon to ascertain what is the law of the case, who is the law-breaker, and how is the law to be kept. You must look out for natural consequences, and effects that follow causes, not for rewards and punishments!

You know that a little bile in the blood may cause great mental distress! But it is perfectly absurd to ask God to save you from these blacks in your eyes and blue devils in your brain. You must look to your liver, and obey the laws of health. Eschew tobacco and take less whisky, or coffee, as the case may be. God works no immediate miracle in response to your offer of a tempting opportunity! He intends man to get rid of evil as he grows enlightened enough to deal more wisely with our human conditions in the process of--what? Of becoming manlier and womanlier.

Our Science grasps with its transforming hand; Makes real half the tales of fairy land;
It turns the deathliest fetor to perfume;
It gives decay new life and rosy bloom;
It changes filthy rags to virgin white,
Makes pure in spirit what was foul to sight.

We burn the darkness and the density out of earthly matter, and transfigure it into glass, which we can see through. We are here to apply a similar process of annealing to our dense, unexcavated, earthy humanity, so that the light from heaven may shine through it purely! We are here to try and clear away these visible causes of obstruction which have been bequeathed to us by ages on ages of horrible ignorance, and not look forward helplessly to their being burned out of human souls by an eternity of hell-fire, or, backwards, for a salvation supposed to have taken place some eighteen centuries ago, but which is no nearer now than it ever was, on the terms set forth by orthodox teachings.

It was impossible to see anything clearly, or get any glimpse of justice above or below, in heaven, or earth, or hell, under the old creed, which proclaims that pain and suffering constitute the curse wherewith God has unjustly afflicted *all* for the sin of one, instead of the beneficent, though stern, angel of his presence and bearer of his blessing: that it was an eternal decree, to be executed through all eternity, instead of an awakener in time, that calls to action now and at once, for the changing of the present conditions in which Humanity crawls, as it were, upon all fours, or hobbles on crutches, as if we were born mental cripples.

We all know there is an awful deal of suffering in the world that cannot be considered as a mere individual question!--sufferings that we do not individually cause, and are not personally responsible for--sufferings bequeathed to us as individuals and as members of the State; for we have to bear the accumulated burdens of centuries on centuries of ignorance, or, worse still, of wilful crime, and, worst of all, of wrong made sacred by religious sanction, and supported by Law and the Press. And the burden of the many crushes the individual to the earth; and the God of Justice appears to be blind to the case--makes no rush to the rescue, even when we suffer for the sins of others. Be sure even these can be turned to eternal account. But, he has this lesson to convey to the world—

Humanity is one. And the power that *is* has instituted certain laws--laws that operate for the species rather than the individual, an important distinction to be made in any interpretation of nature; laws that deal with the species *as one* in spite of our manifold diversities and our deified doctrine of every-one-on-his-own-hook-ism. He does not put forth his hand to take *you* off your hook when it happens to run into you particularly sharp, flesh or soul, and makes you supplicate *or* swear. Establish what private relationship you can with your Maker, and derive what spiritual succour you may whilst bearing the burden, or writhing on the iron that enters you, the laws that do deal with humanity in the aggregate, and operate for the good of the species, *will* go grinding on with their larger revolutions that subserve eternal interests whilst crushing terribly many smaller claims of individual life

For, mark this, the Eternal intends to show us that humanity is one, and the family are more than the individual member, the nation is more than the family, and the human race is more than the nation. And if we do not accept the revelation lovingly, do not take to the fact kindly, why then 'tis flashed upon us terribly, by lightning of hell, if we will not have it by light of heaven, and the poor neglected scum and *canaille* of the nations rise up mighty in the strength of disease, and prove the oneness of humanity by killing you with the same infection.

It has recently been shown how the poor of London do not live, but fester in the pestilential hovels called their homes. To get into these you have to visit courts which the sun never penetrates, which are never visited by a breath of fresh air, and which never know the virtues of a drop of cleansing water. Immorality is but the natural outcome of such a devil's spawning-ground. The poverty of many who strive to live honestly is appalling.

And this disclosure is made with the customary moan that such people attend neither church nor chapel, as if that were the panacea.

I should not wonder if these revelations result in the building of more churches and chapels, and the consecration of at least one or two more bishops.

The Bishop of Bedford said the other day--"It was highly necessary that in these times when the poor have so little earthly enjoyment, the joys of heaven should be made known to them." It is not possible to caricature an utterance so grotesque as that.

How appallingly unjust it seems that the victims of this world's laws should be handed over as ready-made victims of Nature's laws--that the most helpless poor should be the favourite thriving ground for tape-worms--just because they are in such a poverty. This is hard, but so it is, and so it will and must be till the lesson is learned and applied--that the human family is one, and all are bound up together by certain laws willy-nilly; that we are our brother's keeper for all our Cain-like questionings of the fact. We cannot shirk our responsibility; and you are not allowed to get out of the grip of the violated law of the whole, on any pretence of individuality or limited liability. It is we who create the fevers to feed on the poor, when we allow others to get rich by permitting the filth and the poisoned air and water that are sent into the world sparkling with purity; when we allow the rights of property to over-ride the interests of humanity. It is we who breed the diseases and literally invent the hungry, hundred-mouthed tape-worms that get their living out of poverty-stricken blood and hungry stomachs, churning the slime of gnawing emptiness, because we created, or continue, the laws that doom the many to poverty and its parasites of prey.

Providence--that is a very comprehensive name--providence does not create poverty. The cupola of heaven overhead is like the inverted horn of everlasting plenty, pouring down its blessings of abundance in sunshine and shower, in air and dew, in ripening fire and purifying frost, and the harvests never fail the world over. All round, all ways, there is plenty for all--if not in one country, there is in another. There is no failure on the part of Providence, the Creator of plenty.

This neglected garden of our world, which has in it every element of a paradise, if rightly planted and properly tended, has been left to run to weeds of sin and ignorance and crime, in the most wasteful way. Heavens of spirit-worlds around us are for ever sowing the divine seed-germs broad-cast over our earth, and they have to scatter a harvest in order that we may grow a single grain, because the human conditions are so un-receptive, the fields are so neglected, the soil so unprepared to receive their bounty! The heavens around us are ever ready to pour out blessings in a larger measure than we are to make a lap for receiving them. All they ask are the conditions under which we may receive most abundantly.

We are the manufacturers of misery! We have sedulously cultivated or permitted all manner of foul conditions, and then in the midst of some calamity, for which we are criminally responsible, that comes home to all, the praying machine of the State is set rotating with a furious forty-thousand-parson-power, and God is implored to stay his hand or work a miracle forthwith on behalf of us poor human worms, who ask the Creator to take particular notice of these our penitential writhings at his feet! The

Bishop of Truro said recently that we are approaching a period of pain and peril, and the situation calls for strong words and strong prayers. You must cry aloud or the Lord won't hear you!

Standing face to face with certain facts, the result of things as they are, and have been, the atheists exclaim,--"There is no God! If there were an omnipotent God such things would not be tolerated by him!" But by an "omnipotent God," is meant a god with power to change, at a moment's notice, all that is fixed for ever. Let me assure our free-thought friends, that Evolution necessitates a new idea altogether of the operative power! It abolishes the incompetent personal Creator of the Hebrew Genesis! But, in presence of evolution, it is useless to demand that, if there be a God, it shall prove itself to be the deity of the orthodox, which, as I said before, is a sort of eternal weather-cock on the summit of creation, that may be made to veer round as it is blown about by every breath of selfish human prayer, if people collect together in sufficient numbers to blow it round! A vain idea of divinity whosoever entertains it. The deity who is belaboured so unmercifully, and, as I think, so cheaply, by Robert Ingersol, is the god of the non-evolutionary theory of creation, the impossible monster of the past.

"Did God govern America when it had four millions of slaves?" asks Ingersol. Well, why not? in accordance with the Laws of Evolution, seeing that slavery has come to an end! If he had put an end to it, *ab extra,* Americans could not have had the credit of doing the work, and might never have evolved the consciousness that slavery was criminal.

God did not put an end to slavery as an outside Governor of Men; but who shall say that the power, the will, the perception, the affection, or whatsoever we can express by analogy with the human--that is called God--was not operant, and, therefore, governing, within the souls of the men who rose up foremost in revolt against the accursed wrong, and called upon their fellows to cast it out? Possibly the existence of God, then, does not depend upon the particular visible way of working that may be so easily indicated! Slavery only existed *pro tem,* to come to an end, and, therefore, was consistent, like other educational forms of evil, with the divine government, according to the laws of evolution.

The argument of the non-theist is continually directed and limited to the false premises and inadequate conclusions of the orthodox, which it is as easy and cheap to pulverise as it is to pummel a sack of straw! We can know nothing of an omnipotent God who plays fast and loose with the conditions of law! Were it so, all human foothold and trust in the stability of the universe would be gone. Education would be impossible. We are first taught by means of the fixed facts, in order that we may found on solid earth, not on the ever-shifting sands--with prayers for God to catch them now and again, and keep them quiet, *for God's sake!* I rather think it would be more just to reply, there is not sufficient manhood and intelligence in you to put an end to the evils you deplore! *"I, God! gave the earth for all;"* and you permit the initial iniquity of absolute private property in land, whereby one man may clutch a county all to himself, and a few may claim a country. You allow the rights of property to over-rule and over-ride the interests of humanity!

If your national property is doubling every thirty years, so is the national pauperism! You allow the "one" to possess the soil, and the thousands to be driven off and exported as refuse, in order that game may multiply, and the human parasites of earth may pursue their savage sport! I gave the land for all; to be the property and grazing ground of each living generation brought to birth; and you allow it to be locked up by the dead hand of the past, for the benefit of the few! These few framed the laws that inevitably doom the many, sooner or later, to poverty, to man-made sufferings, to diseases and miseries innumerable, all of which get mixed up with a supposed inscrutable origin of evil and other grotesque and fallacious views, endorsed and inculcated by the current theology for the benefit of parsons and patrons, which are only fit to be made a mock of, and to be laughed into oblivion!

And here, let me say, that whilst recognising the inexorableness of the natural law in certain spheres of operation, where it works like the bound Samson of blind force for the good of the species, I find that Spiritualism introduces a consciousness akin, and, at least, equal, to the human, into the working of law in a realm beyond the immediately visible. It shows the existence of subtler forces and modes of law for dealing with man the individual, and the culminating consciousness of creation. When the mind of man had been evolved on this earth, remember, a new factor was introduced amongst the natural forces--one that was destined to greatly modify and counteract them; fetter the fire, and ride the ocean waves; guide the lightning, and train it to carry messages; bridge the planetary spaces, and outstrip Time itself. In like manner, the knowledge of an existence beyond the visible present--no matter by what means--and of intelligence operating in hidden and extraordinary ways, introduces a new factor among the forces now to be reckoned with as mental modifiers in certain domains of law. The unseen world can no longer be the same when we learn that Intelligence is there; no more than this world could remain the same after the advent of man! And when we can identify the consciousness *there* as being akin to the human *here*, we know all that is necessary for putting a conscience into the previously inexorable law, and an *eye* into the image of blind force. Here we get a margin that would take a long while to fill in with possible annotations. Man is no longer alone in the universe! There are other intelligences, affections, powers of will and work, beside his; and in relation to him this just makes all the difference in the manifestation and interpretation of the law that *is* blind and inexorable in its lower range. We begin to distinguish! Here are the means for a possible response to invocation, and to the need of mental help!

The now demonstrated fact of Thought-Transference, which was familiar enough before, in common with other kindred phenomena, to many of us, opens up a vista of immortal possibility in the mode of mental manifestation, and in the modification of supposed hard-and-fast, or immutable, law, in relation to life in its higher phases!

It seems to me that this fact alone turns the ground of mere materialism into a kind of Goodwin Sands! We extend this thought-transference upwards or round us by means of living telegraphic mental lines! The operators on which at one end can work, and only work according to the conditions at the other end. At present I do not perceive, and cannot pretend to know, when and where we can touch Conscious Source itself along these lines. Who does know anything of God, in the domain of things? or who has any right to pretend to know, or to be paid a salary for pretending to know, anything of God personally, or a personal God? To me the question as to the personality of God is altogether premature. I can wait for a few future lifetimes to find out God.

In a sense it may be "there is no God yet, but there's one coming!" and you will find the saying a profound one if you think it over for a month. We ourselves, of the race of man, are only in the condition of becoming (let us cultivate a becoming modesty!); and such is the human apprehension of the cause of becoming. The eye, as Goëthe has said, can only see what it brings with it the power of seeing; and so, in a sense, a God is not yet, but one is coming. The deity hitherto set up for worship is more or less an effigy of the God of primitive or savage man. If that be a true likeness, why, then, men ought not to become Atheists merely--they ought not to marry and propagate, but commit suicide forthwith! It is such an outrage on all human feeling, this primitive portraiture of Eternal power, that the moral revolt is certain, and the mental result is atheism. I assert that non-theism is sometimes, and in some natures, the necessary revolt of the most inner consciousness against the abortion called God! They shut their eyes altogether to get rid of a representation so unsightly and unworthy; and better is such blindness than much false seeing. I say it is the real Presence operating within that is at war with this hideous sham set up for worship without. I seldom use the name of God myself in speech or writing now, it has been so long taken in vain--so profaned by the orthodox blasphemers. It has been so degraded as a brand and hall-mark, made use of to warrant the counterfeit wares that are passed off upon the ignorant and unsuspecting, who think them genuine so long as they are stamped with that name, as to have become quite discredited.

For myself, I have come to apprehend a Conscious Source of all, working outwardly from the core of things, by means of what we term matter, and understand as the Laws of Evolution. A Conscious Source of all! I cannot state that consciousness in words, but it appears to me that this is the work of phenomena which do actually state it in the process of appealing to, or becoming, the Consciousness in us. But I am utterly unable to personify this Power! Also, I find the essence of the whole matter is sacred to privacy. The more intuition, the less blabbing--the more reverence, the more reticence. The facts of an abnormal or extraordinary nature that came under my own cognisance during many years of my life, which were continually occurring and verified, proved to me that Mind exists and operates out of sight!

By degrees these facts peopled the unknown void with life and intelligent beings; that finally gave one bit of foothold on the very first step of a ladder which will stand up for the first time when one tries to prop it against the sky! That one step bridges the dark void of death for me. I don't trouble myself, for myself, about the other world at all--that's all right, if we are! It is for this world people need to be helped. Life is not worth living if we are not doing something towards helping on the work of this world. It is only in helping others that we can truly help ourselves. And we have reason to think that myriads of those who have already left this life with false hopes of salvation are only too glad to help themselves by coming back and helping us to carry on the work of this world.

It is only when we pass out of the domain of self, that the unseen helpers can steal in upon us, and help us as Agents for those who are Agents for others, and so on and on, until the whole vast universe is filled and quick with modes and motions, and forms of being all athrob with subtly-related life; all radiating from central source to uttermost limit; all unified in one eternal consciousness, in which the soul of man, full statured and full-summed, may possibly become conscious that it touches God at last, as a presence, a power, a principle, and may then be made aware that it did so unconsciously from the first.

Our orthodox teachers in the present are responsible for playing into the hands or claws of the devil that was created for them in the past. They are the consecrators of all the ignorance, robbery, and wrong! In England the sinister army of forty thousand men in masks, as it has been truly termed, is paid from the national revenue to act the part of a secret Sunday police! Their chief representatives are the obstructives of sane and humane legislation to-day as ever. A man can't marry his wife's sister because of them.

At the debate on the Pigeon Bill in the House of Lords, some time since, not a single bishop was found to lift up his voice on behalf of the poor dumb and miserably-murdered doves. Not a man was to be found behind any one of the aprons! Every bishop present in the House voted against opening the Museums and Picture Galleries on Sunday! They say, in effect, If you won't come to church, d--n you! you shan't go anywhere else, if we can help it! They want to stand just where they have always stood, at the end of the long dark passage through which mankind slowly emerges out of darkness into day--in the very entrance of the light, to shut out the face of heaven itself from those who are groping their way through the gloom, and bid them in God's name to go back and religiously keep to the obscurity of the cave, if they would be saved!

Each Sunday they trail the red herring across the scent of their followers, so that their attention may be drawn off from this world and all the wrongs we are sent here to remedy. They promise that those who remain sufficiently poor and wormlike in spirit during this life, shall rise erect from the grublike condition in death, full-fledged, to soar as winged angels in the next life. They have exalted the lot of Lazarus as a Scriptural Ideal for the most needy and miserable to live up to, as if the cowering outcast and diseased starveling of earth were the proper model man for the heavens. They keep us the lying farce of insisting that man is a fallen creature, and persist in preaching their doctrine of his degradation and damnation in order that people may go to them to be saved--and pay well for it.

The Secularist asserts that the orthodox cult and theology are a hopeless failure for this world, and as a Spiritualist I affirm that they are also a fraud for the other.

False beliefs are, and forever must be, opposed to all real and true doing. And these false beliefs have from the beginning been bitterly opposed to every truth revealed by science; and every advance made for humanity has had to be made in spite of them. Moreover, this doctrine they teach, of saving yourselves and "devil take the hindmost," is most miserably degrading to any true sense of real manhood or womanhood. He wouldn't be much of a hero who in the midst of the battle took it into his head that the first duty of man is to get himself saved!

They get up a horrible hullabaloo in the rear, as if all hell were let loose after you, on purpose to frighten the blind and foolish, and make them rush through the one door open in front of those who are fleeing from the wrath to come, at which they take tax and toll. But there is no hell, there is no devil, close after the hindmost of those who are furiously fleeing from the avengers of the "fall of man." Moreover, it's of no use rushing. However fast you go you carry your own heaven or hell inside of you, whether for this life or any other. All this is a bogus business, with the mythical devil for bogey. The world is not yet on fire with the final conflagration, nor can they set it on fire with the painted flames of a pictorial hell. A little girl was once asked what she must first do to be saved; and the innocent replied, "Get lost." Moreover, before we join in the stampede of self-salvation at the call of those who cry "fire" when the theatre is crammed, let us be sure that we have grown a soul that is worth saving. If we had, I doubt whether we should manifest such a consuming anxiety of utter selfishness, or be in such an infernal hurry to get it saved anyhow. Those who are truly desirous of saving or helping others, seldom trouble much about their own souls.

Theirs is the burden of a nobler care. Theirs is a loftier inquietude than any sense of self can ever give. They lose all such unworthy fears for themselves in the thought of others. They are like that grand captain of the "Northfleet," of whom I proudly wrote some years ago—

"Others he saved. He saved the name
Unsullied, that he gave his wife,
And, dying with so pure an aim,
He had no need to save his life."

I also hold their other cowardly doctrine, that of vicarious sacrifice, to be the real, if indirect, cause of Vivisection. It would have been impossible for a nation of animal lovers like the English to tolerate the vivisection of the dog, for example, man's first friend in the wilderness of the early world, his ally in the work of civilisation, unless the *motor nerve* and conscience of the race had been paralysed by the *curare* of vicarious suffering. The beastly cruelties of its practitioners, which are flaunted in our faces with intent to terrorise the conscience of others, could not have been permitted by men who had not been indoctrinated by the worship of *a vivisecting deity,* whose *victim* was his own son! And these myriads of slowly murdered dogs and rabbits, cats and frogs, cannot have the consolation of knowing that vivisection is salvation, and they are saviours of the human race from the consequences of its own crimes against nature, and sins against self! It is impossible to establish the throne of Eternal Justice by the violation of all that is human, as is fruitlessly attempted on this ground of the orthodox Creed. It is impossible for you to save or serve humanity by sacrificing all that constitutes the essence of humanity, as is done in this portrayal of a vivisecting deity, who is the responsible operator, with his own son for suffering victim. And this victim of vicarious punishment is held forth as a lure to draw humanity toward a father in heaven of such a nature as that! We may depend upon it that this preaching of what is called Christianity, to get a Sunday sensation, or solace out of it--this plunging of the theological poker red-hot into your seventh-day dose of spiritual flip to give it a zest--this using of hell-fire as a persuader, after the manner of the furnace heated beneath the turkeys, which persuaded the poor things to dance to music played in quick time--this weekly whipping of the devil round the stump is, as the Americans say, pretty well played out; there is nothing new to be said. Suppose we go to work and try to *do* something, instead of making ourselves miserable on Sunday, doing nothing but putting ourselves through all the postures and impostures of the orthodox Sabbatical fashion? In future, mankind will not herd together, like terror-stricken cattle in a thunder-storm, to deprecate the wrath of their God, and offer him praise and presents by way of propitiation, and as a bribe for him not to lose his temper! Good God! What an idea of a God! It is precisely the elemental god of Browning's Caliban, and of the primitive savage! In future, I say, men will not look upon it as a sacred duty to herd together, on purpose to praise and glorify their God one day in seven with their psalm of conceit:

"Let all Creation hold its tongue,
While I uplift my Sunday song;"

lest, being a jealous God, he should blight their harvest, or peradventure burst the boiler of the Excursion Train. Nor will men form leagues, religious or otherwise, on purpose to think alike and make all other people think the same. They cannot think alike if they are ever to grow. The lower the type the greater the likeness! The loftier the development the larger the diversity! *That* is the Natural law. We may co-operate to work, but *not* to *think* alike. *That* could never be free-thinking. Nor will mankind henceforth allow their arms to be paralysed for action by being fixed or "bailed up" in the posture of prayer. We say,--It is a farce, a pitiful one, not a laughable one, for you to pray for God to work a miracle for the kingdom of heaven to come, when you are doing all you can, all your lives, to prevent its coming, or doing nothing to hasten its coming. It is the sheerest mockery of

God and man! You were sent here to create the kingdom, to work it out by living that law of love proclaimed as laying down the life in love for others, and the very reason why the kingdom does not come, and cannot come, is because you stand in the way of its coming. And you, and all who think and act as you do, praying for the better day to come, must be swept out of the way in order that it may come.

Get up from your knees and work for it! Take your weapon in hand and fight for it! Turn fiercely on the devil that dogs our own footsteps, and rescue those that fall by the way and succumb to the powers that make for evil. Turn on the devil--not theoretically, but practically, having ascertained the work that needs to be done. Turn on the devil, not singly, but associated together for doing, instead of believing and talking and praying for God to do! What the Eternal Worker asks of us, as I apprehend the whole matter, is that we shall become conscious co-workers with him in carrying out the divine purposes in proportion as we can make them out! He does not want us to be fear-bound and devil-driven slaves! Not beasts in blinkers, not laggers behind, forever probed by the goad of sheer and sharp necessity; not blind obeyers of his sternest laws that go grinding on willy-nilly, hauling and hurling us along with them in their incessant, vast revolution! but seers of his work, intelligent interpreters of his will, and sharers in his life and love.

In conclusion. There is no origin of evil in the moral domain that is not derivable from ignorance. "The wickedness of a soul," said Hermes, "is its ignorance;" and there is no devil in the moral domain except in the devilish determination to *do* the wrong or *permit* the wrong to be done, after we have evolved the consciousness that recognises the right!

The reason then why God does not kill the devil is because man has unconsciously created or permitted all that is the devil finally; and here or hereafter he has to consciously destroy his own work, and fight himself free from the errors of his own ignorance. Not man the individual merely, but man as part of the whole family of universal humanity. Not man as mortal simply, but as an immortal, standing up shoulder to shoulder, and marching onward step by step and side by side with those who are our elders in immortality, and who still unite with us, and lend a hand to effect in time the *not* altogether inscrutable, but slowly-unfolding, purposes of the Eternal.

www.ingramcontent.com/pod-product-compliance
Lightning Source LLC
Chambersburg PA
CBHW071752090426
42738CB00011B/2666